THE NIGHT BEFORE SERIES™

The Night Before Jesus Fed Five Thousand Men

Written by: Timothy Penland
Illustrated by: Mary Alice Ramsey

cane creek publishers

dawson media®

'Twas the night before Jesus
Fed five thousand men
Plus their wives and their mothers
And lots of children.

The village was quiet
The streets were all dark.
You could hear the trees rustle
You could hear a dog bark.

Inside of one cottage,
the oven was hot
You could smell loaves of bread,
and fish in a pot.

A small boy was sleeping,
beside of his brother
They slept on a mat,
right next to their mother.

He knew that tomorrow
Would be a great day
"Jesus is coming"
He'd heard someone say.

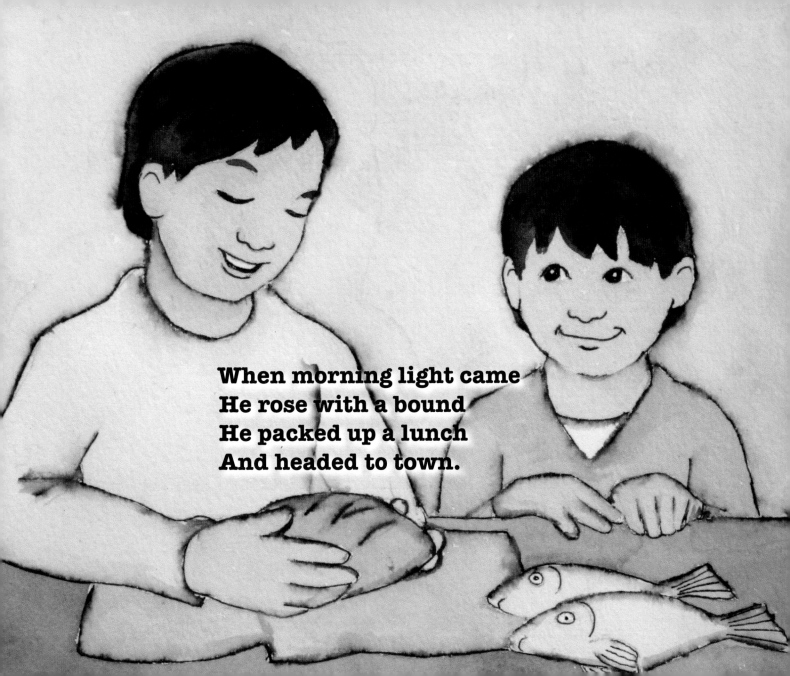

When morning light came
He rose with a bound
He packed up a lunch
And headed to town.

On a hill near the city
He saw a large crowd
There were hundreds and hundreds
Some talking loud.

Down near the shoreline
He thought he could see
Jesus of Nazareth
Down on one knee.

He heard Jesus saying
Let children come
So he ran down the hill
And got closer than some.

Jesus told lots of stories
He said to be kind
He said you should love God
With heart, soul and mind.

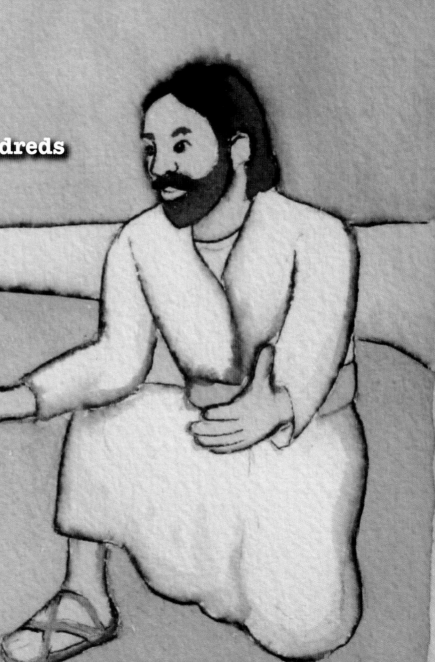

After a long time
His friends said let's leave
But Jesus did something
They couldn't believe

He said, "Have them sit down
Let's just feed them all"
They cried, "We have nothing
And night will soon fall!"

Then Jesus replied
"Bring whatever you find"
They did what he asked
Not knowing His mind

When they came back they'd gathered
The little boy's food
Five loaves and some fish
It did not look good.

They could not imagine
How Jesus could feed
All of the people
With all of their need.

But Jesus just blessed
The little boy's sack
Then said, "Now go feed them
And bring what's left back!"

The disciples took baskets
Now filled to the brim
Fed all of the people
And came back to Him.

They still had twelve baskets
Of fresh fish and bread
That Jesus had blessed -
And thousands were fed.

Jesus taught us two lessons
That day on the sand
The first is to give Him
What we have in our hand.

He'll take it and bless it
In ways we can't see
He'll use what we give Him
He wants you and me.

He also was telling
His friends on that day
That children are special
Don't drive them away.

He loves all the children
Each boy and each girl
No matter what color
Or where in the world.

He told us His Kingdom
Was open to all
Who seek Him as children
And answer His call.

That boy and his lunch
A long time ago
Helped so many people –
A fact you now know.

So take what He gives you
And give it right back,
He'll use any thing
Even fish in a sack.

This book tells a story I have known since I was a very young child. My parents were constantly striving to find new and imaginative ways to make the stories out of God's Word come alive and be memorable to me and my siblings. This book is written in honor of the life and memory of my Dad – Nathan Penland, Sr., and the continuing life and influence of my Mother – Sallie Penland.

Acknowledgements

Thanks are once again in order for the creative group at Cane Creek Publishers who has brought this work to life. Joy, Ben, and Kirk have each added their magical and imaginative skills. Mary Alice's illustrations are awesome and her spirit is infectious. Friends at Fairview Elementary School and other family members and friends have all shared their insight and encouragement to the project.

Timothy Penland

© 2010 by Timothy Penland

Dawson Media and the Dawson Media logo are registered trademarks of NavPress. Absence of ® in connection with marks of Dawson Media or other parties does of indicate an absence of registration of those marks.

ISBN: 978-1-93565-103-1

Library of Congress Control Number: 2010923113

Illustrations by Mary Alice Ramsey
Cover and Interior Design by Kirk Hawkins

Printed in India

1 2 3 4 5 6 7 8 / 14 13 12 11 10